Improve yourself
while in jail or prison

by C. Mahoney

Life is about choices....

You have a choice, today, right now, this very minute, to improve yourself or to stagnate, to learn and explore and try new things and experience what life has to offer you, or you can remain where you are and become nothing more than just a lump of flesh sitting on a bunk. Decide. Yes or no? If you want to become something that others will admire, then turn the page and begin your journey in this book. Read each prompt, once, and again. Think about it, maybe talk with someone else, see what they think, listen, argue, wonder. Then write down your thoughts, the ideas that come to you after wrestling with the question, after engaging it in real life with effort and reason. You know that improving yourself takes effort, work, sweat and resistance. You should be tired when you finish, mentally, and just maybe, spiritually. Turn the page, if you dare.

Is it okay to hate someone, to despise someone who harmed you, a cop, a lawyer, a stranger bunked nearby, a guard that hates you?

_____
_____
_____
_____
_____
_____
_____
_____
_____
_____
_____

_____
_____
_____
_____
_____
_____

What makes you sadder, words that your _friends_ say or words that _strangers_ do NOT say?

_____

_____

_____

_____

_____

_____

_____

_____

_____

_____

_____

_____

_____

Is this place a <u>safe place</u> to be for your emotions, your feelings, or is it a place of anger and frustration and never-ending demands?

_____

_____

_____

_____

_____

_____

_____

_____

_____

_____

_____

_____

_____

_____

_____

_____

_____

Where would you go, if you could, to <u>escape</u> the demands and expectations and necessities of your life, a place to <u>relax</u> and free your mind?

_____

_____

_____

_____

_____

_____

_____

_____

_____

_____

_____

_____

_____

_____

_____

_____

_____

What kind of a person <u>scares</u> you? Not a specific person, but a type of person with particular personality or social traits?

_____

_____

_____

_____

_____

_____

_____

_____

_____

_____

_____

_____

_____

_____

_____

Look within and find those elements that the fires of life have scorched. Eliminate that which is no good, that which provides no heat, that which brings suffering and despair each day. Look within, my friend. Look within.

Does <u>death</u> frighten you, not death at a very old age after you've experience much, but an unexpected and youthful end to all that could be?

_____
_____
_____
_____
_____
_____
_____
_____
_____
_____
_____
_____
_____
_____
_____
_____
_____

Have you ever felt like someone was _watching_ you, maybe from a dark corner or from far away or on a hidden camera?

When were you frightened, really, really scared of someone, what they might _say_ or _feel_ or _think_ about you?

_____

_____

_____

_____

_____

_____

_____

_____

_____

_____

_____

_____

_____

_____

Do you _bully_ other people, friends, strangers, or newbies who show up scared and unsure of what lies ahead of them?

_____

_____

_____

_____

_____

_____

_____

_____

_____

_____

_____

_____

_____

_____

_____

_____

_____

_____

_____

Have you ever <u>dreamed</u> that you were on fire and couldn't put out the flame?
Where do such horrible nightmares come from?

_____

_____

_____

_____

_____

_____

_____

_____

_____

_____

_____

_____

_____

_____

_____

_____

Fire

Your words are powerful, leaving behind scars that won't heal just because you are gone.
Be careful what you say.
Think about why you ask or accuse or coerce, what you have to gain from the pain you cause to others.
Think of how they will feel after the words have had time to dig within and scrape and cut.

Has someone that you love _died_ in your presence, with you right there beside them or in the next room?

_____

_____

_____

_____

_____

_____

_____

_____

_____

_____

_____

When the police put you in handcuffs, who _visited you_, _listened_ to you, _helped_ you to come to grips with your new reality?

_____

_____

_____

_____

_____

_____

_____

_____

_____

_____

_____

_____

_____

What if someone could tell your _future_ just by looking at the lines in your hand. Would you want to know what hasn't happened yet?

_____
_____
_____
_____
_____
_____
_____
_____
_____
_____
_____
_____

_____
_____
_____
_____
_____

Does evil exist, as a thing or in an act that someone does, like a <u>darkness</u> or <u>power</u> or <u>entity</u> that invades humans in times of peril?

_____

_____

_____

_____

_____

_____

_____

_____

_____

_____

_____

_____

_____

_____

_____

_____

_____

Is war good or evil, the <u>killing</u> of people you never met, <u>taking</u> their land and possessions, glorifying and justifying their <u>destruction</u>?

Are you brave? How would your parents react if you told them that you are gay or <u>lesbian</u> or not sure what <u>gender</u> you identify with?

_____

_____

_____

_____

_____

_____

_____

_____

_____

_____

_____

_____

_____

_____

_____

_____

She will miss you now that you are gone. She will be sad and lonely. She will cry, but will she wait? Have you given her a reason to be patient? Have you given her a hope that is real, a hope that will come true, a hope that will bring a smile to her face once again? You control your own destiny, my friend, in the words you say, in the promises you keep, in the kindness you show her.

Is there such a thing as love, or is it really something else like _desire,_ selfishness, or _wanting_ to have something?

_____

_____

_____

_____

_____

_____

_____

_____

_____

_____

_____

_____

Why do so many people dream about flying, at night while asleep? Is this a look into the <u>past</u>, or the <u>future</u>, or something from deep <u>within</u>?

What is the worst thing that someone you are related to did in your presence, something _mean_, something _cruel_, something _selfish_?

_____

_____

_____

_____

_____

_____

_____

_____

_____

_____

_____

_____

                        _____

                        _____

                        _____

                        _____

                        _____

What big secret does your family keep <u>quiet</u> about, the proverbial elephant in the room that everyone does not want to get out in the open?

The darkness
of the night
surrounds
those who
walk alone,
grabbing,
holding,
instilling
fear in those
unable to bear its weight.

The moon provides light to those willing to venture into the beyond, offering a gentle nudge to those who want to see, supporting the walk of those who are fearless.

Don't be afraid to walk, my friend. Don't be afraid.

When is _too much_, too many to feed, too many to occupy the Earth, and will people stop over-populating before it is too late?

_____

_____

_____

_____

_____

_____

_____

_____

_____

_____

_____

Do you ever close your eyes, sitting quietly and thinking of nothing so that your mind and body can find _relief_ from jail's never-ending cacophony?

_____

_____

_____

_____

_____

_____

_____

_____

_____

_____

_____

_____

_____

_____

_____

Is there something or someone that keeps returning to your mind, but you know that they are <u>dangerous</u> and should be forgotten?

_____

_____

_____

_____

_____

_____

_____

_____

_____

_____

_____

_____

                                                                         _____

                                                                         _____

                                                                         _____

                                                                         _____

                                                                         _____

Is it okay to <u>kill</u> someone? Ever? In anger or fear? Soldiers kill strangers in other lands. Police officers kill citizens here. Is that okay?

_____

_____

_____

_____

_____

_____

_____

_____

_____

_____

_____

_____

_____

_____

_____

Let go!

Free yourself from the expectations of those who see only what is
on the surface.

Run! Jump! Fly!

Today is your day to become who you were meant to be.

Did you do everything you could possibly do today? You know, of course, that you can't live today again. It's over. Did you use your __time__ wisely?

_____

_____

_____

_____

_____

_____

_____

_____

_____

_____

_____

_____

_____

_____

_____

_____

What makes you _happy_ and how long does this emotion last? Why can't it last for long periods, days, weeks, our entire life?

_____

_____

_____

_____

_____

_____

_____

_____

_____

_____

_____

_____

_____

_____

Is it okay to kill other living creatures, and then eat them, just because we're _bigger_ and _faster_ and _smarter_...and they taste yummy?

_____

_____

_____

_____

_____

_____

_____

_____

_____

_____

_____

_____

                                    _____

                                    _____

                                    _____

                                    _____

                                    _____

Is presenting yourself in a way that draws attention to you and your body the best use of your _intellect_ and _creativity_?

_____

_____

_____

_____

_____

_____

_____

_____

_____

_____

_____

_____

_____

_____

What keeps you balanced, healthy, sane? What holds the thoughts within and gives you strength to endure the storms of life? Don't be fooled by the immediateness of those who want your attention and laughter and support. Focus on what is good for you, what is healthy, what will bring about growth and change and peace.

Is _hurting_ another person okay, even if both of you agree? Is that showing respect for another person's body, or your own?

_____

_____

_____

_____

_____

_____

_____

_____

_____

_____

_____

_____

_____

_____

_____

_____

_____

_____

Can you _trust_ a police officer to tell you the truth, a sheriff, a deputy, a guard?

_____

_____

_____

_____

_____

_____

_____

_____

_____

_____

_____

_____

_____

_____

Do you realize that <u>one day</u> you will be hearing less, forgetting more, and choosing to sit rather than stand or walk or run?

_____

_____

_____

_____

_____

_____

_____

_____

_____

_____

_____

_____

_____

_____

_____

_____

_____

_____

Is it fair to others, your family or friends who visit you, or strangers you are stuck beside, to be in a bad mood?

_____

_____

_____

_____

_____

_____

_____

_____

_____

_____

_____

_____

_____

_____

_____

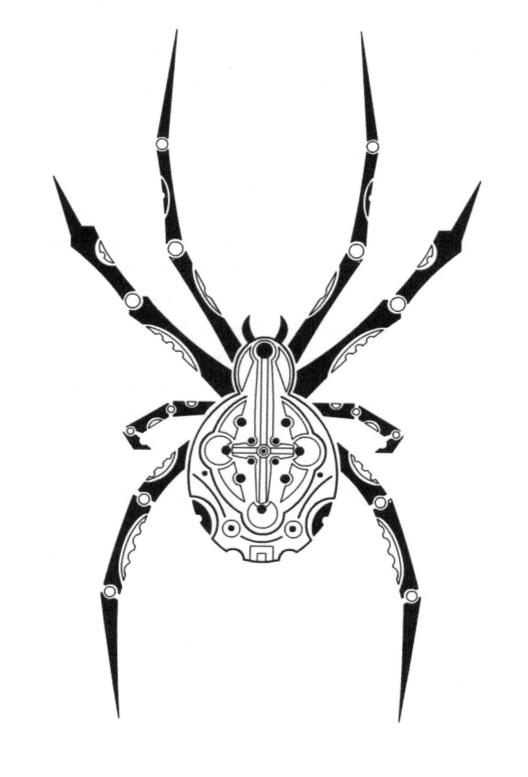

Why should you obey sometimes, not all of the time, but <u>some times</u>?

_____
_____
_____
_____
_____
_____
_____
_____
_____
_____
_____

                          _____
                          _____
                          _____
                          _____
                          _____
                          _____

How do you cope with <u>boredom</u>, the monotony of life, the drudgery, when you know you'd rather be doing something else?

_____

_____

_____

_____

_____

_____

_____

_____

_____

_____

_____

_____

_____

Is it fair to expect someone else to <u>clean up</u> after you?

_____

_____

_____

_____

_____

_____

_____

_____

_____

_____

_____

_____

_____

_____

Do you _help_ out before someone asks you, noticing things that need to be done and doing them on your own?

_____

_____

_____

_____

_____

_____

_____

_____

_____

_____

_____

_____

Is <u>beauty</u> important, how you look, your hair, your skin, your eye color, your cheek bones, your chin?

_____

_____

_____

_____

_____

_____

_____

_____

_____

_____

_____

_____

If someone driving a car kills another person, by accident or by bad choices, should they go to prison? Why? How does that help the *victim*?

_____

_____

_____

_____

_____

_____

_____

_____

_____

_____

_____

_____

_____

_____

_____

People use guns to <u>hunt</u> animals, to <u>hit</u> targets or cans or bottles, and to <u>kill</u> other people.   Is there a bad way to use a gun?

_____

_____

_____

_____

_____

_____

_____

_____

_____

_____

_____

_____

_____

_____

_____

_____

Do you <u>own</u> anything, really own it? What gives you the right to call something, a present or purchased item, yours?

_____

_____

_____

_____

_____

_____

_____

_____

_____

_____

_____

_____

_____

_____

_____

_____

Walk the path with those who are searching for peace, and if you cannot find anyone, then walk alone.

Are the stories you hear as a child, like the flood or the creation story, real?
Did they really happen or are they meant to <u>teach</u> an eternal truth or moral?

_____

_____

_____

_____

_____

_____

_____

_____

_____

_____

_____

HOLY BIBLE

_____

_____

_____

_____

_____

_____

Is day better than night, more fun, more meaningful, more adventurous, more exciting?

_____
_____
_____
_____
_____
_____
_____
_____
_____
_____
_____
_____
_____
_____
_____
_____
_____

How did the _Earth_ come to be, the planet itself and its roundness and travelling through space and rockiness and wateriness?

_____

_____

_____

_____

_____

_____

_____

_____

_____

_____

_____

_____

_____

_____

_____

_____

Do aliens exist, out there in the far reaches of the universe, in our galaxy or in other galaxies, _living_, _thinking_, _moving_ around?

_____

_____

_____

_____

_____

_____

_____

_____

_____

_____

_____

_____

_____

What did you leave behind?

Is it okay to spend billions of dollars on a space program when there are children around the world in need of food, shelter, clothing and education?

_____

_____

_____

_____

_____

_____

_____

_____

_____

_____

_____

_____

_____

_____

_____

Why do storytellers depict the <u>snake</u> as evil or self-centered or lying?

_____

_____

_____

_____

_____

_____

_____

_____

_____

_____

_____

_____

_____

_____

_____

Who do you look at as a good person, someone you admire, someone you respect, someone who did kind acts for others?

_____

_____

_____

_____

_____

_____

_____

_____

_____

_____

_____

What is it about _music_ that makes us want to dance or jiggle our body or snap our fingers or bob our head without caring what people think?

_____

_____

_____

_____

_____

_____

_____

_____

_____

_____

_____

_____

_____

Who is the worst person that has ever existed, and why do you say that this person is _evil_ or _bad_ or _horrible_?

_____

_____

_____

_____

_____

_____

_____

_____

_____

_____

_____

_____

_____

_____

_____

_____

_____

_____

Can you believe the _news_ you watch on television?

_____

_____

_____

_____

_____

_____

_____

_____

_____

_____

_____

_____

_____

_____

Is what _man_ crafts better than what _nature_ creates?

_____

_____

_____

_____

_____

_____

_____

_____

_____

_____

_____

_____

_____

_____

_____

What makes a _church_ a good organization and not just another business that collects money from visitors in order to pay people's salaries?

_____

_____

_____

_____

_____

_____

_____

_____

_____

_____

_____

_____

_____

_____

_____

_____

What is it about prayer that gives many people peace when all around them a storm pushes and attacks and hurts?

_____

_____

_____

_____

_____

_____

_____

_____

_____

_____

_____

_____

_____

_____

_____

Is it <u>responsible</u> to expect God or an angel or someone on earth to pull you out of your misery and bring a smile to your face?

_____

_____

_____

_____

_____

_____

_____

_____

_____

_____

_____

_____

_____

_____

_____

_____

MY GOD IS AN AWESOME G✝D

Why do big fish eat small fish? Isn't that bad? If they can do it, then why can't big humans eat small humans?

_____

_____

_____

_____

_____

_____

_____

_____

_____

_____

_____

_____

_____

                        _____

                        _____

                        _____

                        _____

                        _____

                        _____

What is _wrong_ about sneaking into a theater to watch a movie that you did not pay for? Or is that okay?

ADMIT ONE

Rage builds up in a fiery explosion.

Resentment follows to lead the mind toward justification.

Revenge brings a moment of relief.

Ruin follows like a shadow.

When does _life_ begin, at the moment a chick cracks its egg, or while it is a liquid inside of an egg, or at another moment before all of that?

_____

_____

_____

_____

_____

_____

_____

_____

_____

_____

_____

_____

_____

_____

_____

_____

Why are some activities so much fun when we are small children, but we never do them again once we become adults?

_____

_____

_____

_____

_____

_____

_____

_____

_____

_____

_____

_____

_____

Why do people on Earth speak so many languages? Is one language better than the others? Should we get rid of all the other languages except one?

_____

_____

_____

_____

_____

_____

_____

_____

_____

_____

_____

SE
HABLA
ESPAÑOL

_____

_____

_____

_____

_____

_____

Will we ever reach a stage where a robot has the same rights as a human?
What reason will we use for denying or giving them equal rights?

_____

_____

_____

_____

_____

_____

_____

_____

_____

_____

_____

_____

_____

_____

_____

_____

Pause for a moment.

Take a deep breath.

Imagine the pain escaping.

Start over.

When does a child obtain the special rights and privileges that adults have?
Why must a child wait until a certain age before they have control?

_____

_____

_____

_____

_____

_____

_____

_____

_____

_____

_____

_____

_____

_____

_____

_____

If we should treat all people as if they are the same, then why do some people get A's and other people get F's in school?

_____

_____

_____

_____

_____

_____

_____

_____

_____

_____

_____

_____

_____

_____

How does knowledge help a person live a happier life?

_____

_____

_____

_____

_____

_____

_____

_____

_____

_____

_____

_____

_____

_____

_____

Why do adults create candy that tastes delicious, yet they tell kids not to eat too much candy? Isn't that a little hypocritical?

_____

_____

_____

_____

_____

_____

_____

_____

_____

_____

_____

_____

_____

_____

Regret comes. I try to ignore it. I lie to myself, hoping to feel better, but I lose the battle because it won't leave me alone. I know what I did. I know. I did it. I was wrong.

What makes you sad, so sad that you must turn away from others so that they do not see your tears?

_____

_____

_____

_____

_____

_____

_____

_____

_____

_____

_____

What does your mind do as you sleep at night? Does it rest, or does it wander through fields of weirdness and wonder seeking entertainment?

_____

_____

_____

_____

_____

_____

_____

_____

_____

_____

_____

_____

_____

Why do many people look upward when they are trying to think of something they don't know, or when they are lying?

_____

_____

_____

_____

_____

_____

_____

_____

_____

_____

_____

Close your eyes and the world disappears. Have you ever wished that you could do the same thing with your ears so that you could enjoy the silence?

_____

_____

_____

_____

_____

_____

_____

_____

_____

_____

_____

_____

_____

When is it a bad time to monkey around, to act silly or goofy?

_____

_____

_____

_____

_____

_____

_____

_____

_____

_____

_____

                          _____

                          _____

                          _____

                          _____

                          _____

                          _____

Do all lives matter, or just those who look like you and speak like you and are from the same area as you and are as angry as you?

_____

_____

_____

_____

_____

_____

_____

_____

_____

_____

_____

_____

_____

_____

Why do siblings argue so often?

Is it okay to support a sports team who uses a mascot that promotes an offensive stereotype?

_____

_____

_____

_____

_____

_____

_____

_____

_____

_____

_____

_____

_____

_____

_____

Is it okay to tattoo hate symbols onto your body and expose these to everyone as a means of "free speech"?

_____

_____

_____

_____

_____

_____

_____

_____

_____

_____

_____

_____

                                      _____

                                      _____

                                      _____

                                      _____

                                      _____

                                      _____

                                      _____

Is it okay to tattoo religious preferences or ethnic identities or geographical origins or philosophical visions onto visible parts of our body for all to see?

_____

_____

_____

_____

_____

_____

_____

_____

_____

_____

_____

_____

_____

_____

What if you grew up and learned that the stories of magic and miracles you were told as a child were just that, imaginative stories?

_____

_____

_____

_____

_____

_____

_____

_____

_____

_____

_____

               _____

               _____

               _____

               _____

               _____

Is it okay for a person to hate you because their holy book tells them that anyone who is different is wrong/cursed?

_____

_____

_____

_____

_____

_____

_____

_____

_____

_____

_____

_____

_____

_____

Be the one who goes the other direction, toward success, toward independence, toward relief. Don't follow the crowd.

Are guys smarter than girls, or girls smarter than guys, or what?

Who has the answers, which church, which religion, which philosophy of living?

_____

_____

_____

_____

_____

_____

_____

_____

_____

_____

_____

_____

_____

_____

_____

_____

Are humans more deserving of protection than other life forms, land creatures and sea creatures, diggers and fliers, if you must choose?

_____

_____

_____

_____

_____

_____

_____

_____

_____

_____

_____

_____

_____

_____

_____

_____

_____

Why must you bring a present if you attend a birthday party for a friend or family member, or is love all you need?

_____
_____
_____
_____
_____
_____
_____
_____
_____
_____
_____
_____
_____
_____
_____
_____
_____
_____

That chair you sat in remains empty...

Is it okay for a parent to spank a child?

What does it say about humans that we kill smaller life forms?

_____

_____

_____

_____

_____

_____

_____

_____

_____

_____

_____

_____

_____

Have you ever been in a fight, hitting someone in the face in anger?

_____

_____

_____

_____

_____

_____

_____

_____

_____

_____

_____

_____

_____

_____

_____

_____

Are you racist, in any way, in even the smallest amount, toward people who are darker than you or who speak another language?

_____

_____

_____

_____

_____

_____

_____

_____

_____

_____

_____

_____

_____

_____

_____

_____

Have you ever slept on the floor with no pillow or blanket?

_____

_____

_____

_____

_____

_____

_____

_____

_____

_____

_____

_____

_____

_____

Have you ever eaten no food all day, no breakfast, no lunch, no dinner, and then went to bed with a growling and frustrated stomach?

_____

_____

_____

_____

_____

_____

_____

_____

_____

_____

_____

_____

_____

_____

_____

Have you ever heard something that someone else said, and wished that you hadn't heard it?

_____

_____

_____

_____

_____

_____

_____

_____

_____

_____

_____

_____

                        _____

                        _____

                        _____

                        _____

                        _____

Have you ever seen something while being nosy, and then wished that you hadn't seen it because it was disgusting or just wrong?

_____

_____

_____

_____

_____

_____

_____

_____

_____

_____

_____

_____

_____

_____

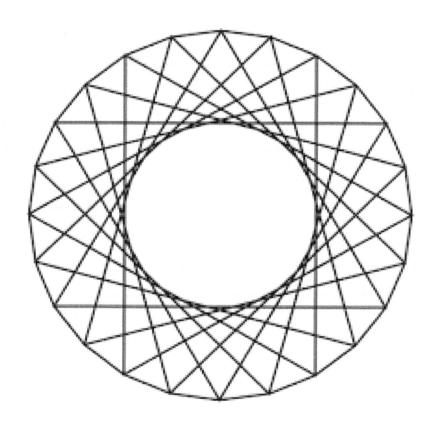

Have you ever had a really good idea, but when you shared it with your friends they just laughed at you?

_____

_____

_____

_____

_____

_____

_____

_____

_____

_____

_____

                              _____

                              _____

                              _____

                              _____

                              _____

                              _____

What makes you smile?

_____

_____

_____

_____

_____

_____

_____

_____

_____

_____

_____

_____

_____

_____

_____

Do you believe in the impossible, in things that science tells you did not happen and cannot happen?

_____

_____

_____

_____

_____

_____

_____

_____

_____

_____

_____

_____

_____

_____

_____

_____

_____

_____

Are people good or bad, or both, or neither?

_____

_____

_____

_____

_____

_____

_____

_____

_____

_____

_____

_____

_____

Have you give thought to what you will do, how you will be different, why a new course is necessary?

Is there something that you would never do because it is wrong?

_____

_____

_____

_____

_____

_____

_____

_____

_____

_____

DO NOT ENTER

_____

_____

_____

_____

_____

What is your favorite game?

_____

_____

_____

_____

_____

_____

_____

_____

_____

_____

_____

_____

_____

If you could live forever, would you, and what age would you want to be, a kid, a teenager, a young adult, a parent, a grandparent?

_____
_____
_____
_____
_____
_____
_____
_____
_____
_____

                          _____
                          _____
                          _____
                          _____
                          _____
                          _____

How do you decide who to love and who you hate, who you hang out with and who you will avoid, who you talk to and who you ignore?

_____

_____

_____

_____

_____

_____

_____

_____

_____

_____

_____

_____

_____

_____

Choices

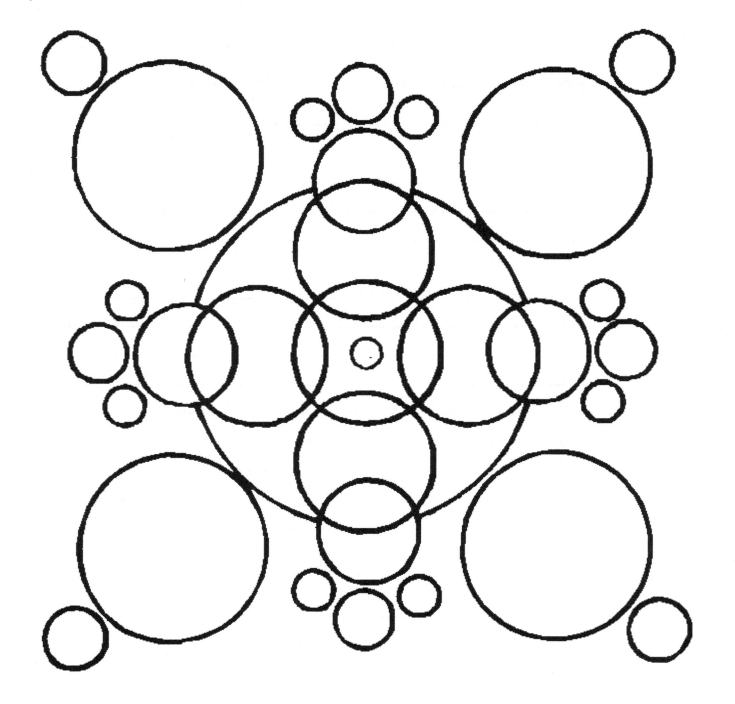

When do you prefer to be by yourself, alone?

What do you do when someone is hurting you, or bullying you, or threatening you?

_____

_____

_____

_____

_____

_____

_____

_____

_____

_____

_____

_____

_____

What is your philosophy on life, the main idea that gets you what you want each day?

_____
_____
_____
_____
_____
_____
_____
_____
_____
_____
_____
_____

Yes! I can!

_____
_____
_____
_____
_____
_____

Whose fault is it when you fail?

_____
_____
_____
_____
_____
_____
_____
_____
_____
_____
_____
_____
_____
_____

🚫 BLAME

This is the moment when you smile, when you turn around and look back at the distance you have travelled, at the height of your ascent, at the length of your climb. You made it, though each step took effort and each obstacle dealt you pain. But with effort comes growth, and with growth comes strength. You have that strength now, the power and endurance and flexibility to handle any problem that comes your way. Take a deep breath and rest your mind. Enjoy a moment of silence as you recognize what you have just done. You did it. Be proud of yourself.

Made in the USA
Monee, IL
08 November 2019